Easy Piano

Disney's
My First Song Book
Volume 4

A TREASURY OF FAVORITE
SONGS TO SING AND PLAY

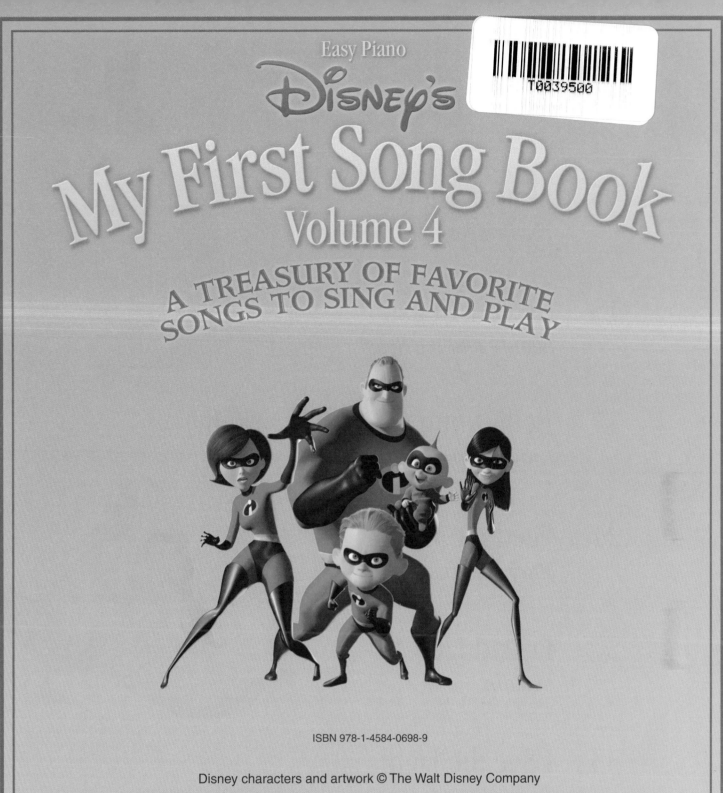

ISBN 978-1-4584-0698-9

Wonderland Music Company, Inc.
Walt Disney Music Company

DISTRIBUTED BY

HAL•LEONARD®

7777 W. BLUEMOUND RD. P.O. BOX 13819 MILWAUKEE, WI 53213

In Australia Contact:
Hal Leonard Australia Pty. Ltd.
4 Lentara Court
Cheltenham, Victoria, 3192 Australia
Email: ausadmin@halleonard.com.au

Visit Hal Leonard Online at
www.halleonard.com

Contents

5 Almost There
The Princess and the Frog

13 Be Our Guest
Beauty and the Beast

17 Bella Notte (This Is the Night)
Lady and the Tramp

21 Feed the Birds
Mary Poppins

27 Friend Like Me
Aladdin

33 I See the Light
Tangled

41 I'm Late
Alice in Wonderland

45 If I Never Knew You
Pocahontas

49 The Incredits
The Incredibles

55 The Medallion Calls
*Pirates of the Caribbean:
The Curse of the Black Pearl*

61 Scales and Arpeggios
The Aristocats

65 So This Is Love (The Cinderella Waltz)
Cinderella

69 True Love's Kiss
Enchanted

77 We Belong Together
Toy Story 3

83 Where the Dream Takes You
Atlantis: The Lost Empire

92 Written in the Stars
Aida

87 You Can Fly! You Can Fly! You Can Fly!
Peter Pan

ALMOST THERE

from Walt Disney's *The Princess and the Frog*

Music and Lyrics by
RANDY NEWMAN

Freely, with motion

Spoken: Mama, I don't have time for dancin'. That's just gon-na have to wait a

while. _____ Ain't got time for mess-in' a-round, _

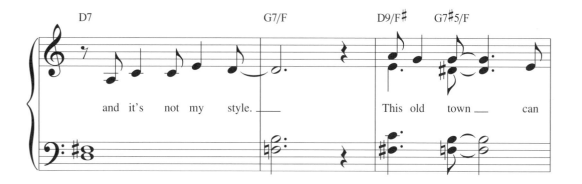

and it's not my style. _ This old town _ can

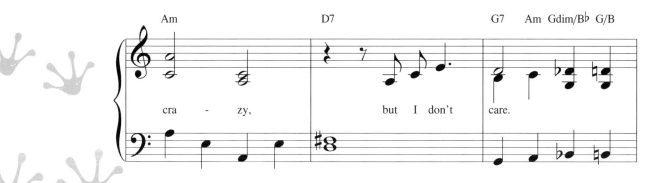

cra - zy, but I don't care.

Trials _____ and trib - u - la - tions, I've had ___ my

share. There ain't noth-ing gon - na stop me now ___ 'cause I'm ___

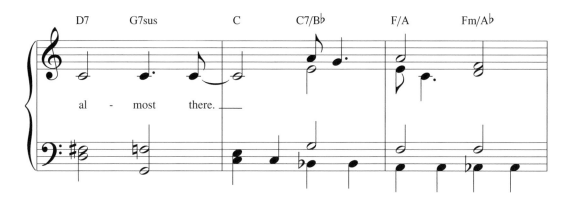

al - most there. _____

C/G   G7#5   C   Cdim

I re - mem - ber Dad - dy

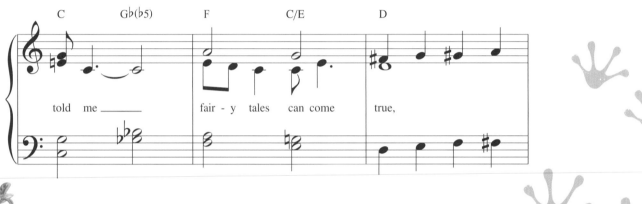

C   G♭(♭5)   F   C/E   D

told me _____ fair - y tales can come true,

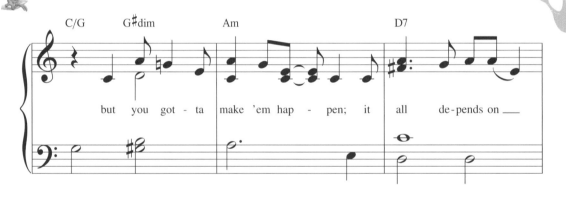

C/G   G#dim   Am   D7

but you got - ta make 'em hap - pen; it all de - pends on ___

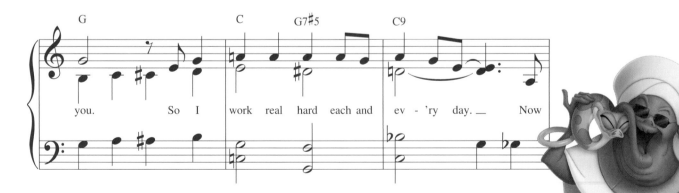

G   C   G7#5   C9

you.   So I work real hard each and ev - 'ry day. ___ Now

8

things for sure ___ are go - ing my way. ___ Just do - ing

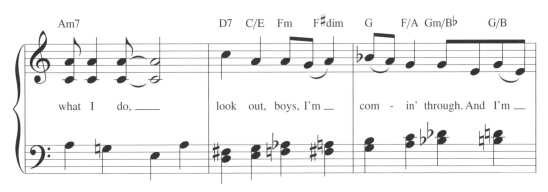

what I do, ___ look out, boys, I'm ___ com - in' through. And I'm ___

al - most there, I'm al - most

there. Peo - ple gon - na come here from ev - 'ry - where, ___ and I'm

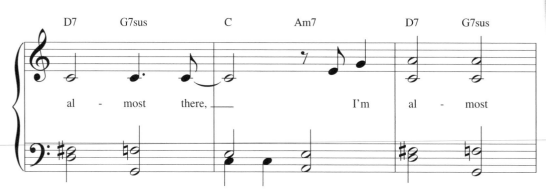

al - most there, _____ I'm al - most

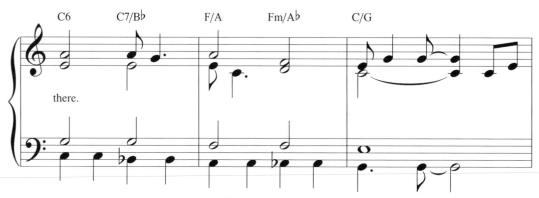

there.

Slower

There've been trials and trib - u - la - tions.

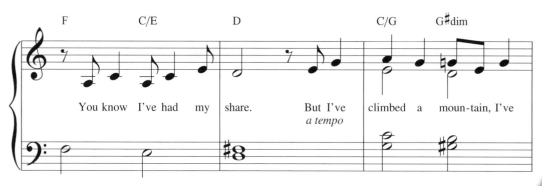

You know I've had my share. But I've climbed a moun-tain, I've

a tempo

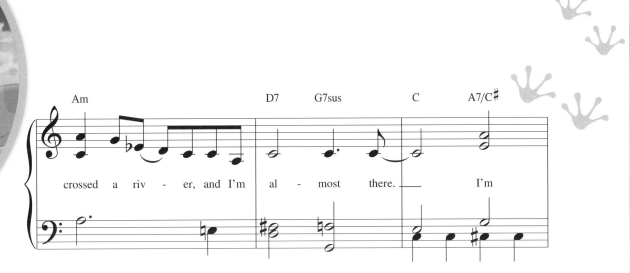

crossed a riv – er, and I'm al – most there. _____ I'm

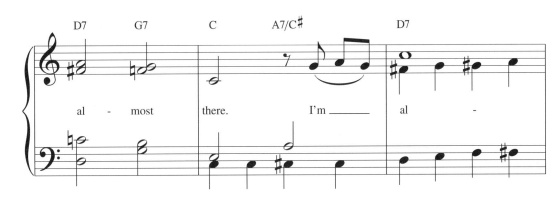

al – most there. I'm _____ al –

most there.

Be Our Guest

from Walt Disney's *Beauty and the Beast*

Lyrics by HOWARD ASHMAN
Music by ALAN MENKEN

Moderately

Be our guest! Be our guest! Put our

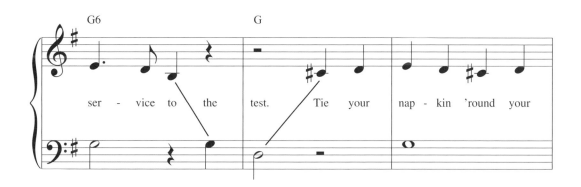

ser - vice to the test. Tie your nap - kin 'round your

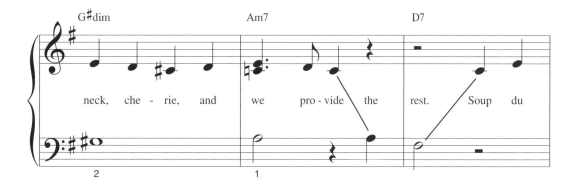

neck, che - rie, and we pro - vide the rest. Soup du

jour! Hot hors d'oeuvres! Why, we on - ly live to

serve. Try the grey stuff, it's de - li - cious! Don't be -

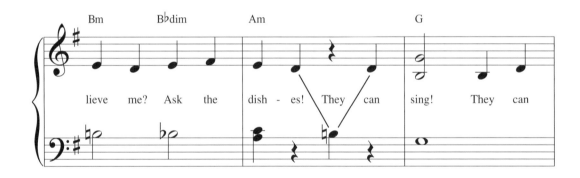

lieve me? Ask the dish - es! They can sing! They can

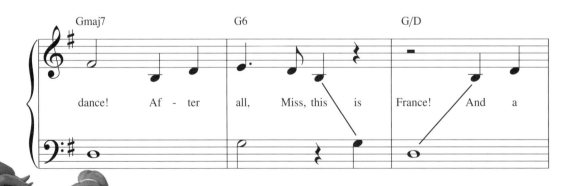

dance! Af - ter all, Miss, this is France! And a

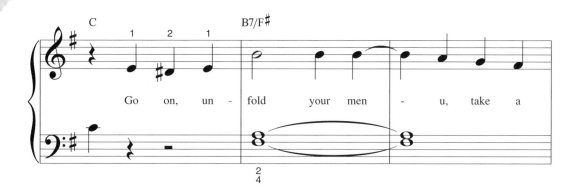

din - ner here is nev - er sec - ond best.

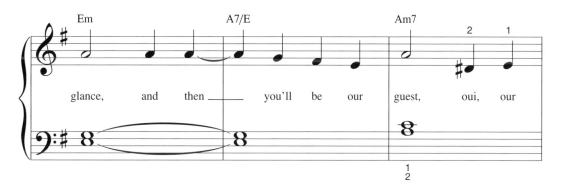

Go on, un - fold your men - u, take a

glance, and then ___ you'll be our guest, oui, our

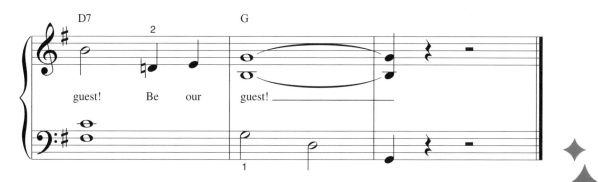

guest! Be our guest! ___

Bella Notte
(This Is the Night)

from Walt Disney's *Lady and the Tramp*

Words and Music by PEGGY LEE
and SONNY BURKE

This ___ is the night, ___ it's a beau - ti - ful night, ___ and we

call it Bel - la Not - te.

Look ___ at the skies; ___ they have stars ___ in their eyes ___ on this

love - ly Bel - la Not - te. So

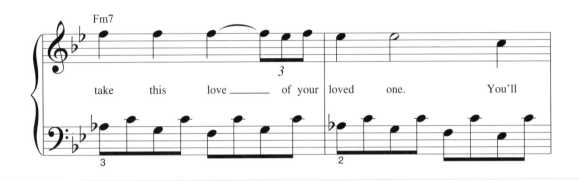

take this love _____ of your loved one. You'll

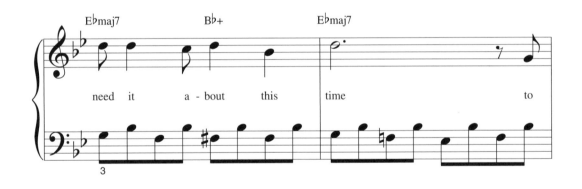

need it a - bout this time to

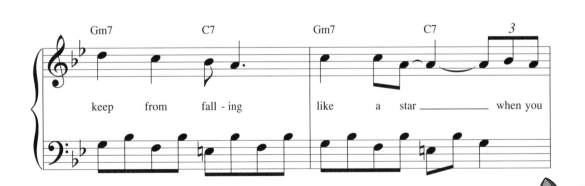

keep from fall - ing like a star _____ when you

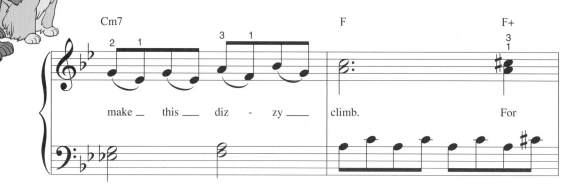

make _ this _ diz - zy _ climb.   For

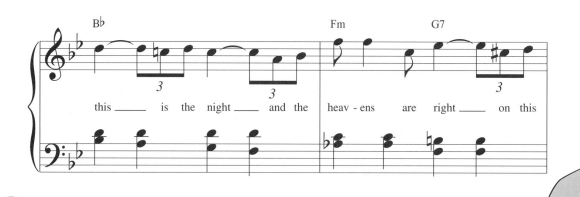

this ___ is the night ___ and the   heav - ens   are   right ___ on this

love - ly Bel - la   Not - te.

rit.   *pp*

Feed the Birds

from Walt Disney's *Mary Poppins*

Words and Music by RICHARD M. SHERMAN
and ROBERT B. SHERMAN

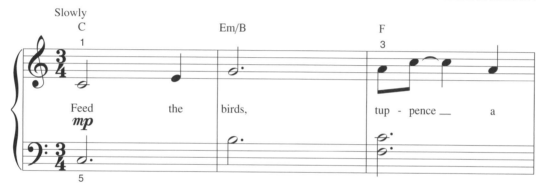

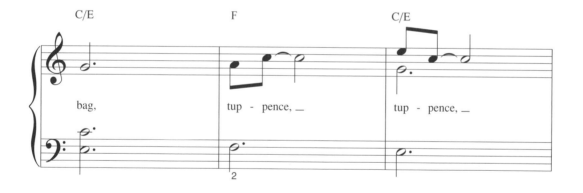

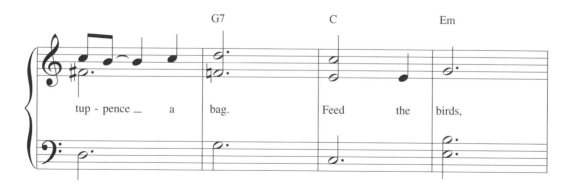

F ... **E7** ... **Fmaj7**

tup - pence __ a bag, tup - pence, __

F#m7b5 ... **C/G** ... **G7** ... **C**

tup - pence, __ tup - pence __ a bag.

E7sus ... **E7** ... **Am** ... **Dm/A**

Ear - ly each day to the

Adim7 ... **Dm/A** ... **Am**

steps of St. Paul's, the lit - tle old

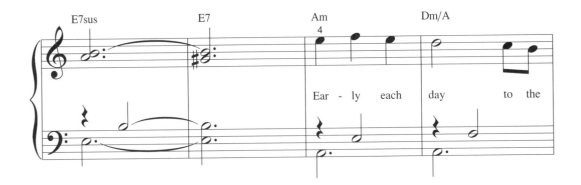
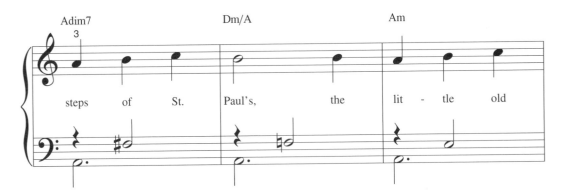

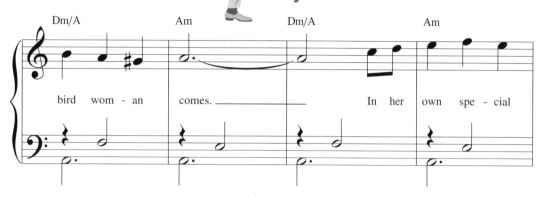

Dm/A   Am   Dm/A   Am

bird wom - an comes. _____ In her own spe - cial

Dm/A   Adim7   Dm/A

way to the peo - ple she calls,

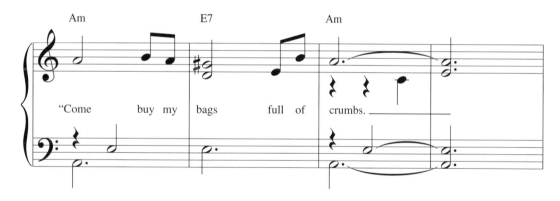

Am   E7   Am

"Come buy my bags full of crumbs. _____

G7   C/G

Come feed the lit - tle birds, show them you care,

G7 · · · · C

and you'll be glad if you do. _____ Their

Am · · · Dm/A · · · Adim7

young ones are hun - gry, their nests are so

Dm/A · · · Am · · · E7

bare. All it takes is tup - pence ___ from

Am · · · G7 · · · C · · · Em/B

you." _____ Feed the birds,

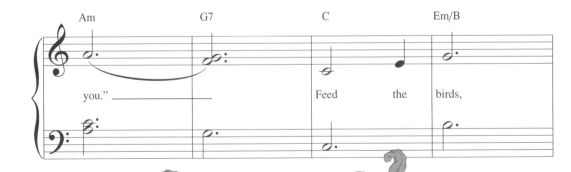

tup - pence __ a bag, tup - pence, __

tup - pence, __ tup - pence __ a bag. "Feed the

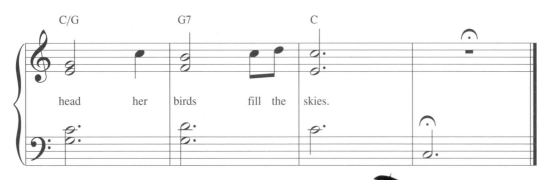

birds," that's what she cries, while o - ver -

head her birds fill the skies.

Aladdin

Friend Like Me

from Walt Disney's *Aladdin*

Lyrics by HOWARD ASHMAN
Music by ALAN MENKEN

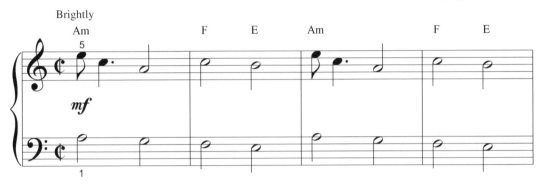

Well, A - li

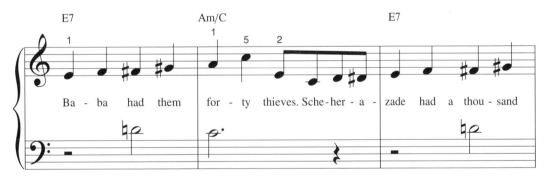

Ba - ba had them for - ty thieves. Sche - her - a - zade had a thou - sand

tales. But, mas - ter, you in luck 'cause up your sleeves you got a

brand of mag - ic nev - er   fails. You got some   pow - er in your

cor - ner now, some heav - y   am - mu - ni - tion in your   camp. You got some

punch, piz - azz, ya - hoo and how. See all you got - ta do is rub that

lamp. And I'll say   Mis - ter A - lad - din, sir, what   will your pleas - ure

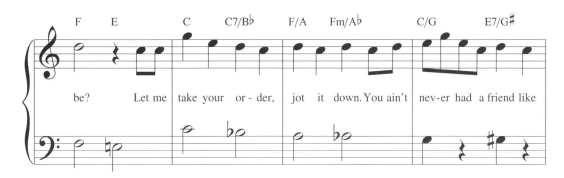

be? Let me take your or - der, jot it down. You ain't nev-er had a friend like

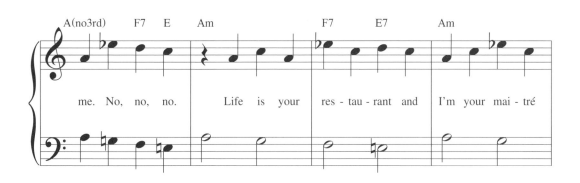

me. No, no, no. Life is your res - tau - rant and I'm your mai - tré

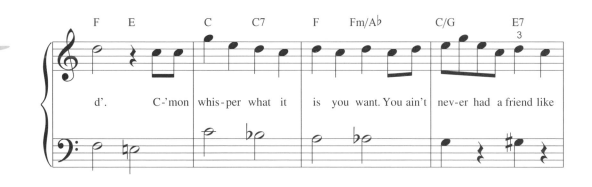

d'. C-'mon whis-per what it is you want. You ain't nev-er had a friend like

me. Yes, sir, we pride our-selves on ser - vice. You're the boss, the king, the

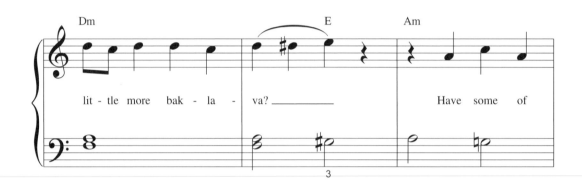

shah. Say what you wish. It's yours! True dish, how 'bout a

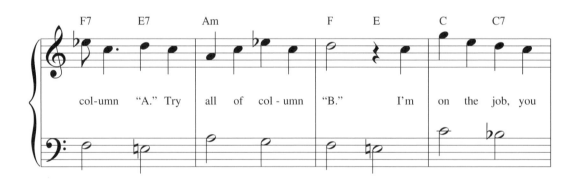

lit - tle more bak - la - va? _____ Have some of

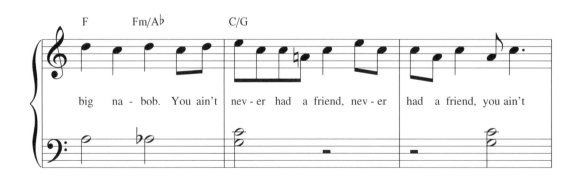

col-umn "A." Try all of col-umn "B." I'm on the job, you

big na - bob. You ain't nev - er had a friend, nev - er had a friend, you ain't

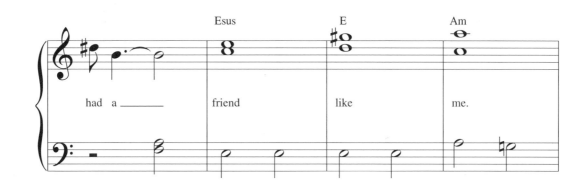

nev - er had a friend, nev - er had a friend. You ain't nev - er _____

had a _____ friend like me.

Wa ah ah. Wa ah ah.

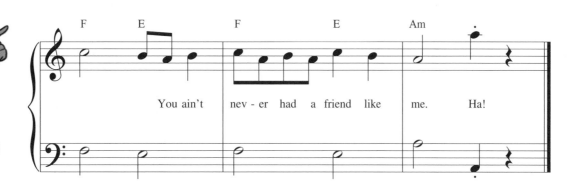

You ain't nev - er had a friend like me. Ha!

I See the Light

from Walt Disney Pictures' *Tangled*

Music by ALAN MENKEN
Lyrics by GLENN SLATER

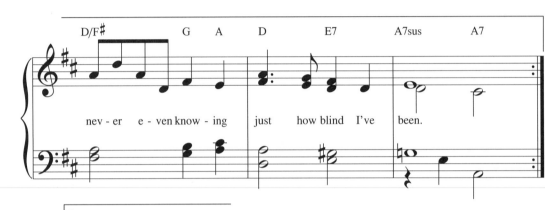

A7/D   D   1. G

out - side,   look - ing   in.   All   that   time,
sud - den - ly I   see.

D/F#   G   A   D   E7   A7sus   A7

nev - er   e - ven know - ing   just   how blind I've   been.

2. G   F#m   Bm7   E7

Stand - ing   here,   it's   oh, so   clear   I'm   where   I'm meant   to

A7sus   A7   G(add2)   G   D(add2)/F#

be.   And   at   last   I   see   the   light,   and it's

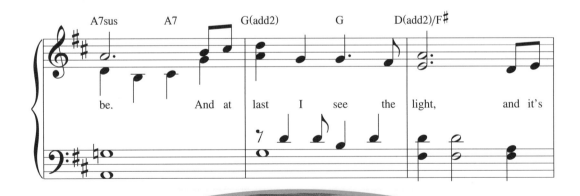

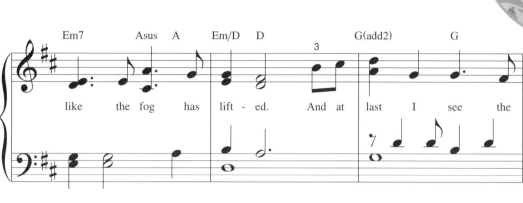

Em7　　　Asus　A　Em/D　D　　　G(add2)　　　G

like　the fog　has　lift - ed.　And at　last　I　see　the

D(add2)/F#　　　F#sus　　F#　　　Bm7

light,　　and it's　like　the sky　is　new.　　And it's

G(add2)　　　　　　D　　　　　　　F#m

warm　and real　and　bright,　　　and the　world　has some - how

G　　　　　　　　　　　　D

shift - ed.　　　　　　　　All　at　once,

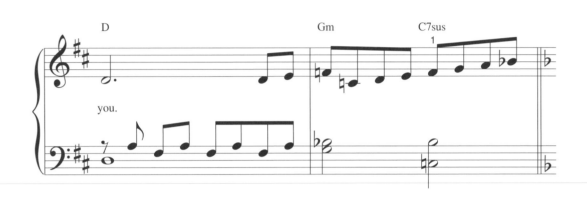

ev - 'ry - thing looks dif - f'rent, now that I see you.

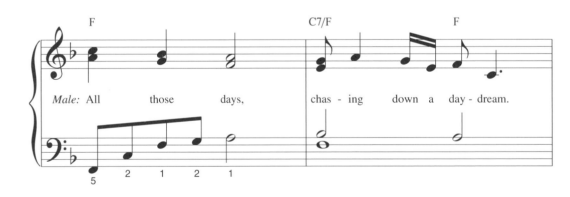

Male: All those days, chas - ing down a day - dream.

All those years liv - ing in a blur. All that time,

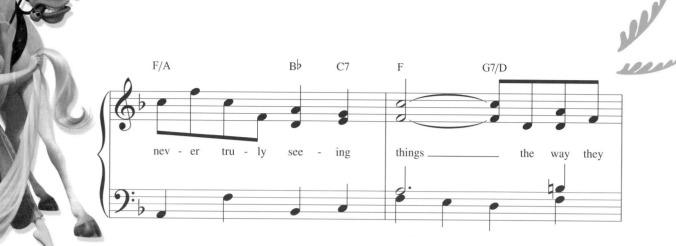

never truly see-ing things _____ the way they

were. Now she's here, shin-ing in the star - light.

Now she's here; sud-den-ly I know:

if she's here, it's crys - tal clear I'm where I'm meant to

go.   *Both:* And at last I see the light,   *Male:* and it's

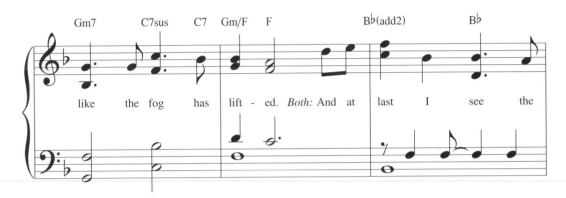

like the fog has lift - ed. *Both:* And at last I see the

light,   *Female:* and it's like the sky is new.   *Both:* And it's

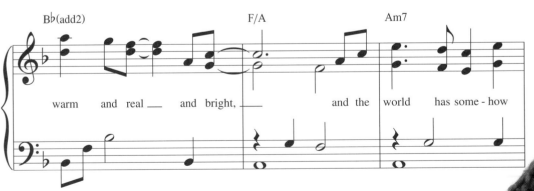

warm and real __ and bright, __ and the world has some - how

shift - ed.

All at once,

ev - 'ry - thing is dif - f'rent,

now that I see you.

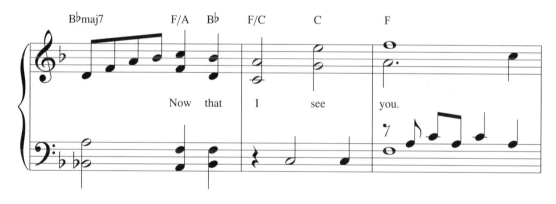

Now that I see you.

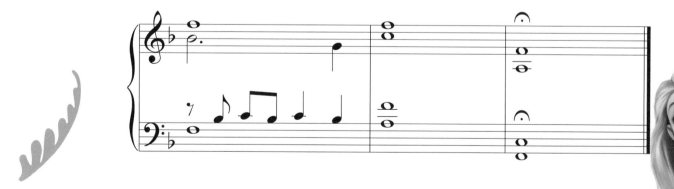

I'M LATE

from Walt Disney's *Alice in Wonderland*

Words by BOB HILLIARD
Music by SAMMY FAIN

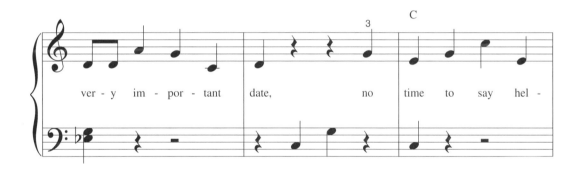

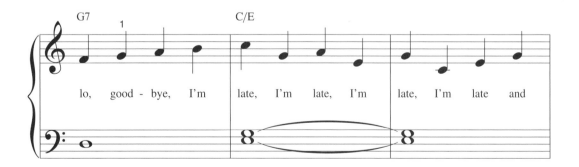

Cm/E♭

when   I   wave   I   lose   the   time   I

2
4

Em   B/D#

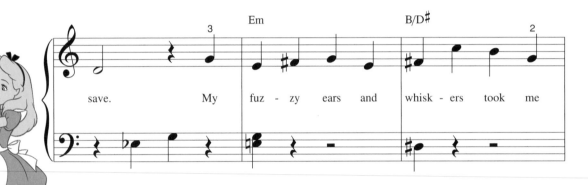

save.   My   fuz - zy   ears   and   whisk - ers   took   me

Em   Am6   Em/G   G7/B

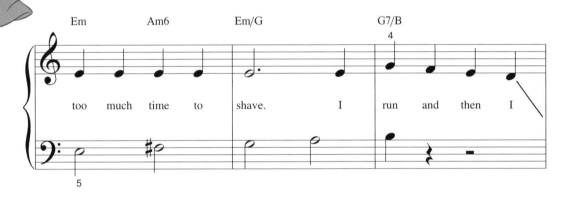

too   much   time   to   shave.   I   run   and   then   I

C   G7/B   C

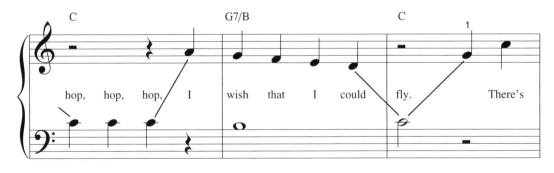

hop,   hop,   hop,   I   wish   that   I   could   fly.   There's

42

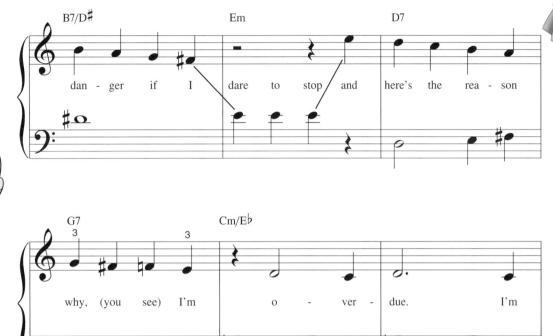

danger if I dare to stop and here's the rea - son

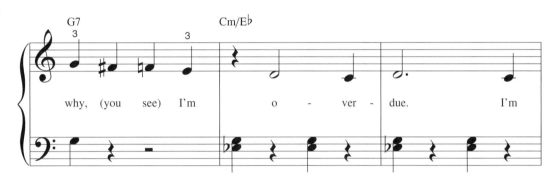

why, (you see) I'm o - ver - due. I'm

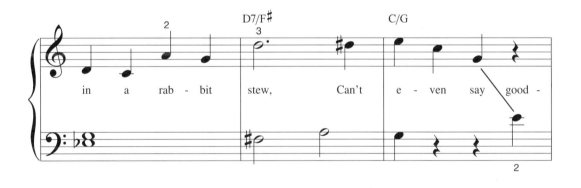

in a rab - bit stew, Can't e - ven say good -

bye, hel - lo, I'm late, I'm late, I'm late.

If I Never Knew You

from Walt Disney's *Pocahontas*

Music by ALAN MENKEN
Lyrics by STEPHEN SCHWARTZ

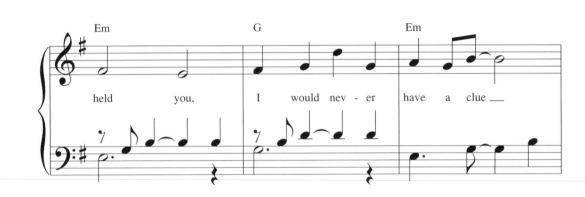

C   D7sus   G

pre - cious life can be.   And if I nev - er

Em   G   Em

held you,   I would nev - er have a clue ___

Am   Cm(maj7)   Cm6   Em   Bm/D

how, at last ___ I'd find in you   the miss-ing part of

C   Am   Cmaj7/D   D7   Am

me. ___   In this world so full of fear, ___   full of rage and

46

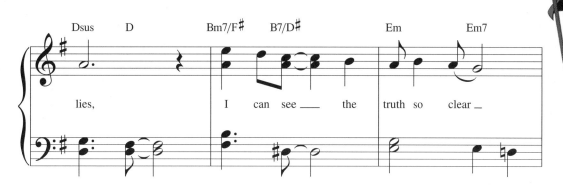

lies, I can see ___ the truth so clear ___

in your eyes, ___ so dry your eyes. ___ And I'm so grate - ful

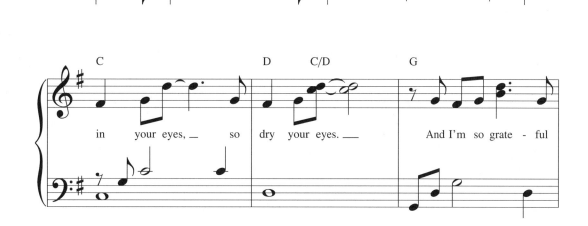

to you. I'd have lived ___ my whole life through,

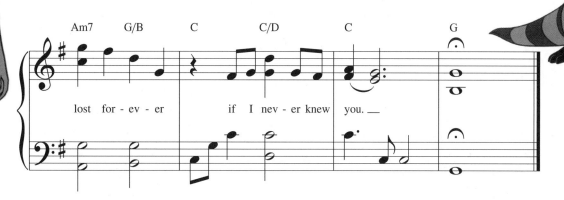

lost for - ev - er if I nev - er knew you. ___

The Incredits

from Walt Disney Pictures'
The Incredibles - A Pixar Film

Music by
MICHAEL GIACCHINO

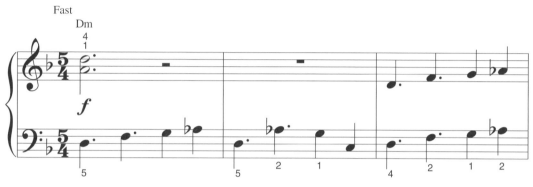

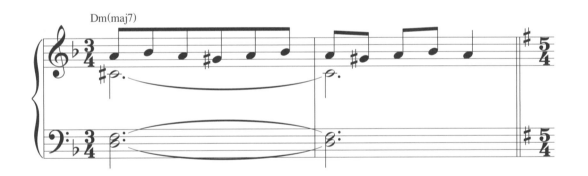

Em6/9

Play 3 times

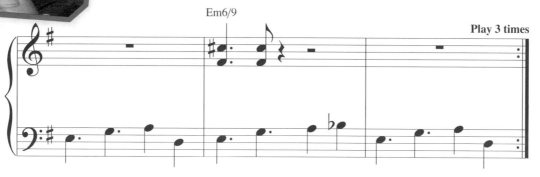

Edim7   N.C.   F/B

Em/B

Em(maj7)

The Medallion Calls

from Walt Disney Pictures' *Pirates of the Caribbean:
The Curse of the Black Pearl*

Music by KLAUS BADELT

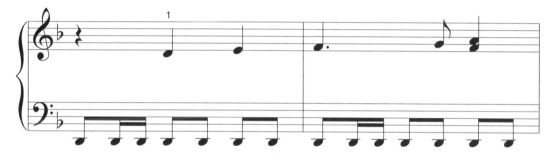

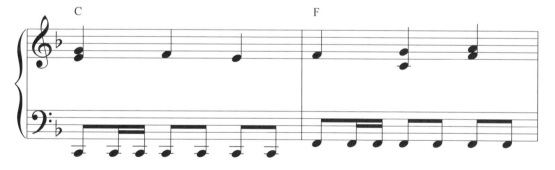

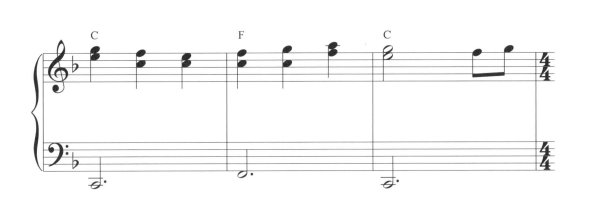

Scales and Arpeggios

from Walt Disney's *The Aristocats*

Words and Music by RICHARD M. SHERMAN
and ROBERT B. SHERMAN

Do mi sol do, do sol mi do.

Ev - 'ry tru - ly cul - tured mu - sic stu - dent knows
If you're faith - ful to your dai - ly prac - tic - ing,
Though at first it seems as tho' it does - n't show,

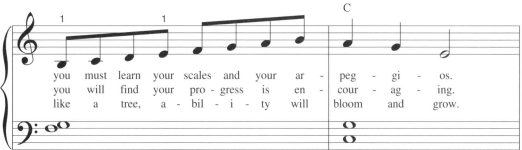

you must learn your scales and your ar - peg - gi - os.
you will find your pro - gress is en - cour - ag - ing.
like a tree, a - bil - i - ty will bloom and grow.

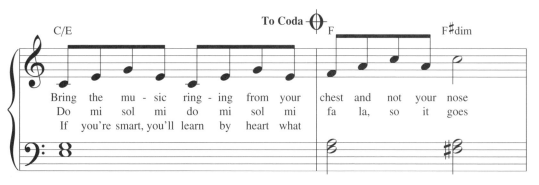

Bring the mu - sic ring - ing from your chest and not your nose
Do mi sol mi do mi sol mi fa la, so it goes
If you're smart, you'll learn by heart what

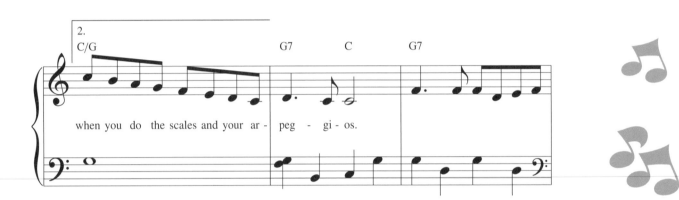

1.
C/G   G7   C

while you sing your scales and your ar - peg - gi - os.

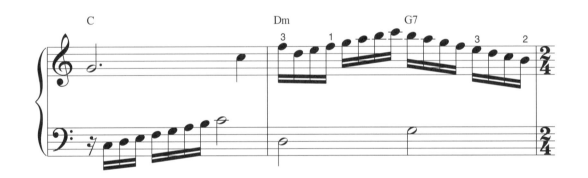

2.
C/G   G7   C   G7

when you do the scales and your ar - peg - gi - os.

C   Dm   G7

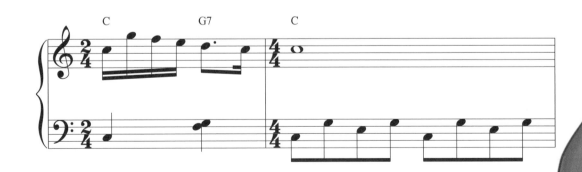

C   G7   C

Do mi sol do, do sol mi do.

D.S. al Coda

Do mi sol do, do sol mi do.

CODA

F   F#dim

ev - 'ry art - ist knows:
rall.

N.C.   G7sus   G7

you must sing your scales and your ar - peg - gi -

C   G7   C

os. _____
a tempo

So This Is Love
(The Cinderella Waltz)

from Walt Disney's *Cinderella*

Words and Music by MACK DAVID,
AL HOFFMAN and JERRY LIVINGSTON

Tenderly

So this is love, (Mm.) _____ so this is

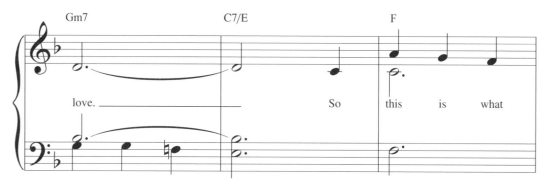

love. _____ So this is what

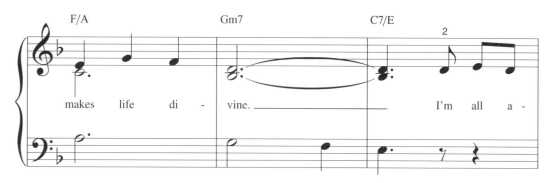

makes life di - vine. _____ I'm all a -

glow, (Mm.) _____ and now I know _____

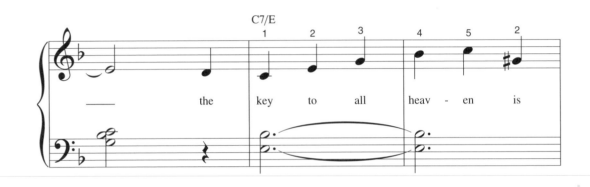

_____ the key to all heav - en is

mine. _____ My heart has wings, (Mm.) _____

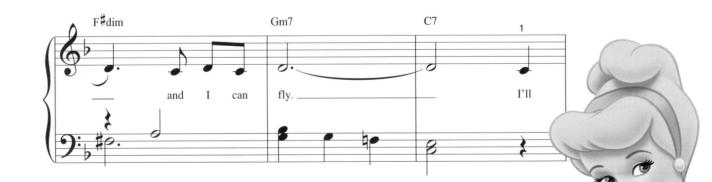

_____ and I can fly. _____ I'll

F/A   F7/A   B♭

touch ev - 'ry   star in the   sky. _____

Gm7   C7

_____ So   this is the   mir - a - cle that
cresc.

F/A   D7/F♯   Gm7

I've been dream - ing   of. (Mm, _____   mm.) _____

C7/E   F

_____ So this is   love. _____

from Walt Disney Pictures' *Enchanted*

Music by ALAN MENKEN
Lyrics by STEPHEN SCHWARTZ

When you meet the some - one who was meant for you, be -

fore two can be - come one, there's some-thing you must do.

There is some-thing sweet-er ev-'ry-bod-y needs.

More flowing, still freely

I've been dream-ing of a true love's kiss;

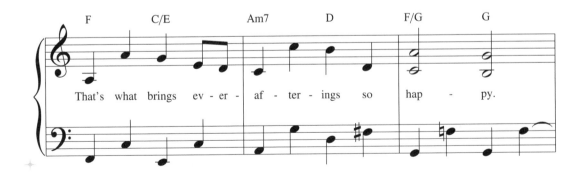

and a prince I'm hop-ing comes with this.

That's what brings ev-er-af-ter-ings so hap - py.

And that's the rea-son we need lips so much,

for lips are the on - ly things that touch. So, to spend a

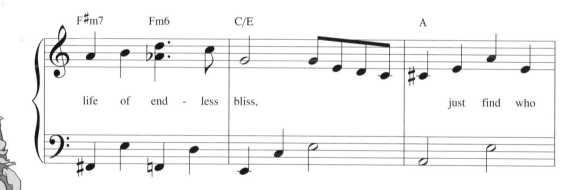

life of end - less bliss, just find who

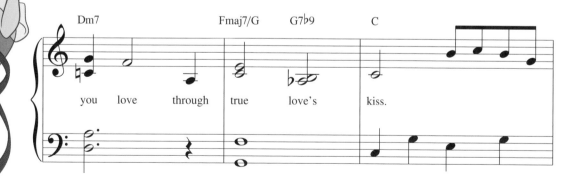

you love through true love's kiss.

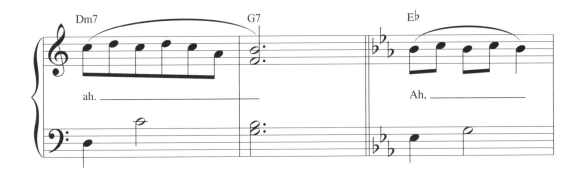

ah, _____ ah. _____

She's been dream - ing of a true love's

kiss, and a prince she's hop - ing

comes with this. That's what

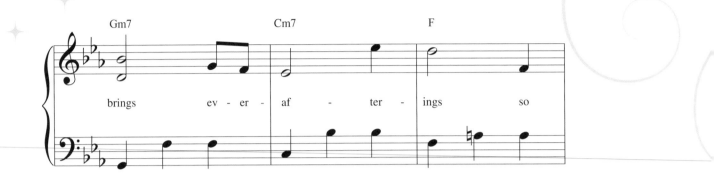

brings ev - er - af - ter - ings so

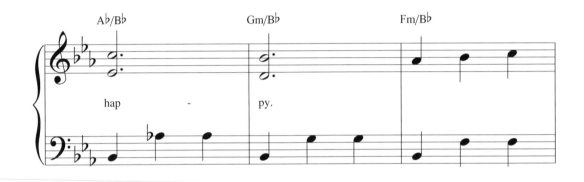

hap - py.

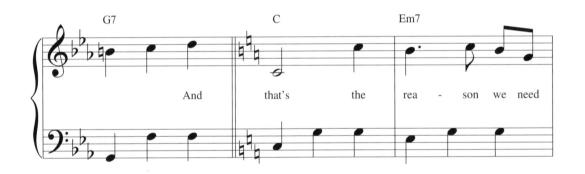

And that's the rea - son we need

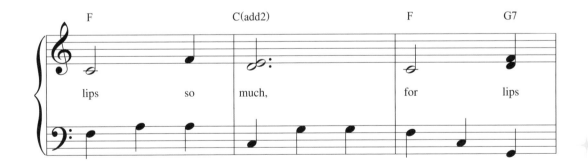

lips so much, for lips

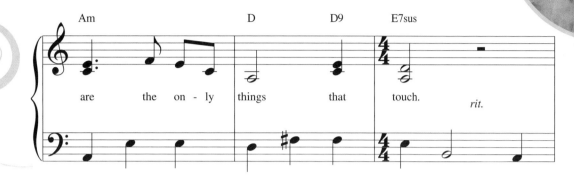

are the on - ly things that touch. *rit.*

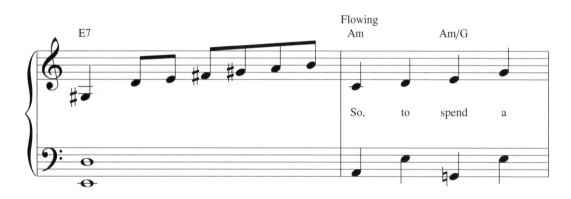

So, to spend a

life of end - less bliss, just find who

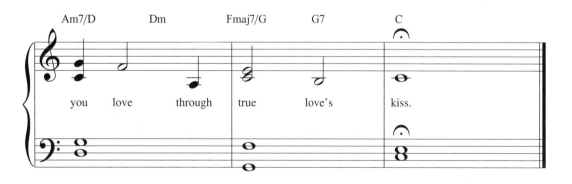

you love through true love's kiss.

75

We Belong Together

from Walt Disney Pictures'
Toy Story 3 - A Pixar Film

Music and Lyrics by
RANDY NEWMAN

Moderately fast

Don't you turn your back on me; don't you walk away.

Don't you tell me that

I don't care, __'cause I do. __

Don't you tell me I'm not the one; __ don't you tell me I

ain't no fun. Just tell me you love me like I love you. You

know you do. __ When we're to - geth - er, __ gray skies

clear up, _____ and I cheer up _____ to where I'm

less de - pressed. _ And sin -

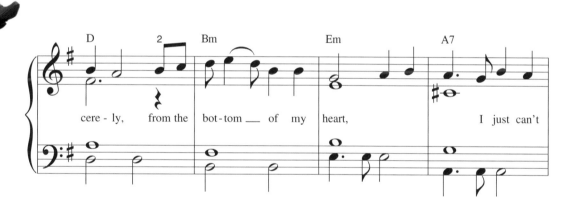

cere - ly, from the bot-tom _ of my heart, I just can't

take it when we're a - part.

We be - long to - geth - er.

We be - long to - geth -

- er, yes we do. You'll be

mine for - ev - er.

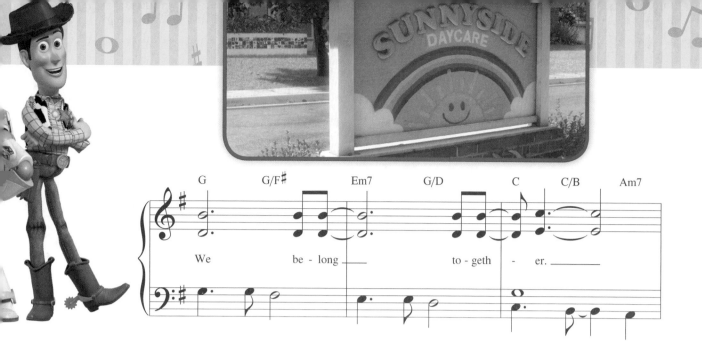

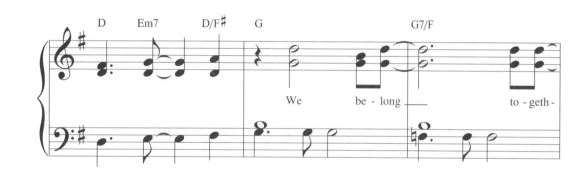

G   G/F#   Em7   G/D   C   C/B   Am7

We   be - long   to - geth - er.

D   Em7   D/F#   G   G7/F

We   be - long   to - geth -

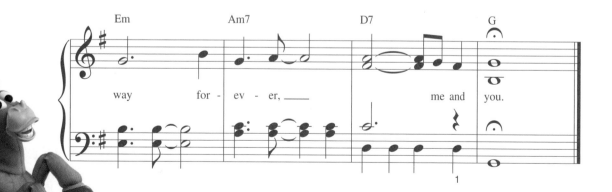

Am7/E   3   Cm6/Eb   G/D

- er.   You know it's   true.   It's gon - na   stay   this

Em   Am7   D7   G

way   for - ev - er,   me and   you.

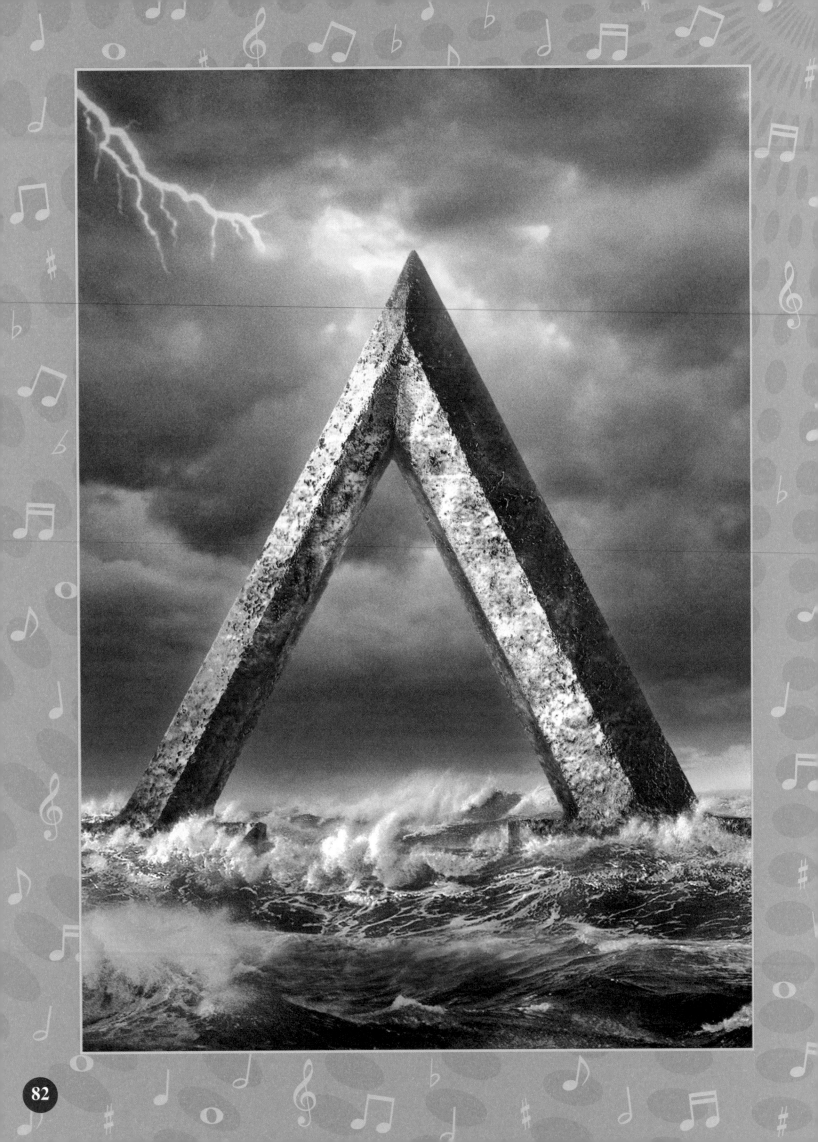

WHERE THE DREAM TAKES YOU

from Walt Disney Pictures' *Atlantis: The Lost Empire*

Lyrics by DIANE WARREN
Music by DIANE WARREN and JAMES NEWTON HOWARD

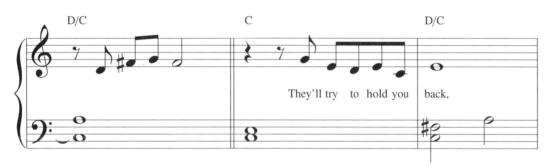

They'll try to hold you back,

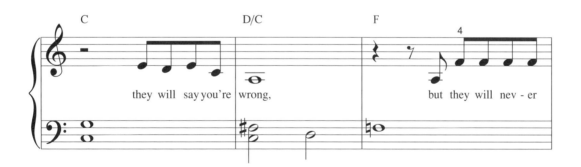

they will say you're wrong, but they will nev-er

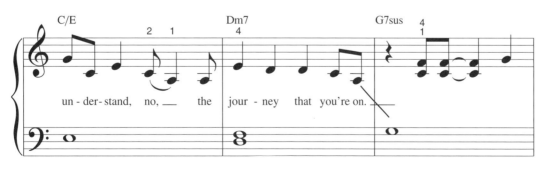

un-der-stand, no, the jour-ney that you're on.

C   D/C   C

They'll try to change your mind;   they'll try to change your

D/C   F   C/E

heart, ___ oh yeah,   but they will nev - er   un - der - stand

Dm7   Em   Fmaj7   C

who you are. And you   still be - lieve ___   (still be - lieve) and

Dm7   C/E

you know   you must go   where the   dream ___ takes you, ___
(and you know)   (you must go)

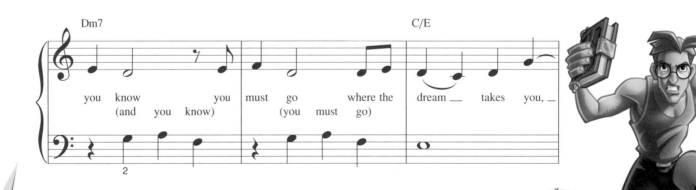

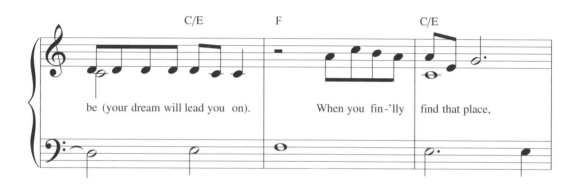

You Can Fly! You Can Fly! You Can Fly!

from Walt Disney's *Peter Pan*

Words by SAMMY CAHN
Music by SAMMY FAIN

Think of the pres-ents you're brought, an - y mer-ry lit - tle

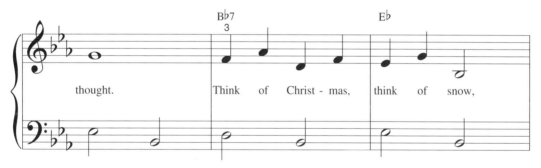

thought. Think of Christ - mas, think of snow,

think of sleigh bells, here we go! Like rein - deer in the

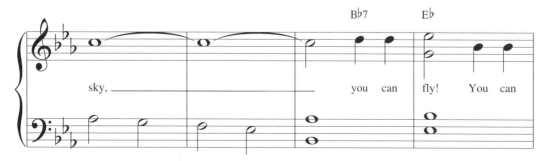

sky, _____ you can fly! You can

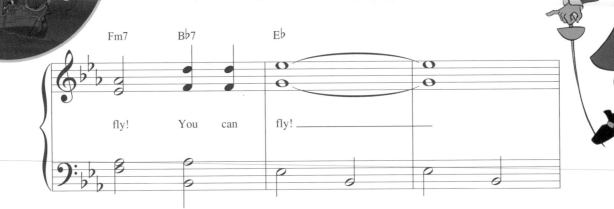

fly! You can fly! _____

Think of the hap - pi - est things, that's the way to get your

wings. Now you own a can - dy store.

Look! You're ris - ing off the floor. Don't won - der how or

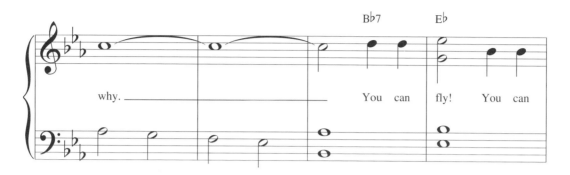

why. _____ You can fly! You can

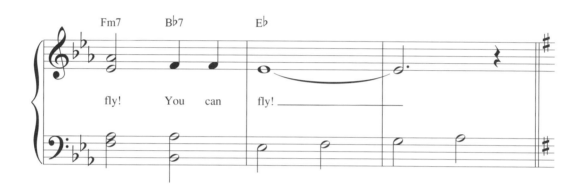

fly! You can fly! _____

Soon you'll zoom all a - round the room, all it takes is faith and

trust. But the thing that's a pos - i - tive must is a

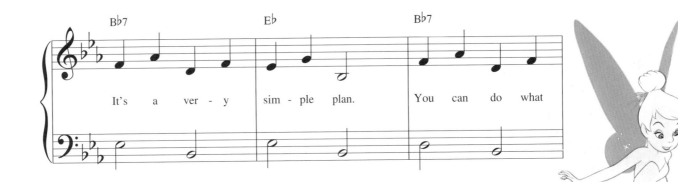

G   Am7   D7   G   Edim   Fm7   B♭7

lit - tle bit of Pix - ie   Dust.   The   dust   is   a   pos - i - tive

E♭

must! _____   When there's a smile in your

heart   there's   no   bet - ter time to   start.

B♭7   E♭   B♭7

It's   a   ver - y   sim - ple plan.   You   can   do   what

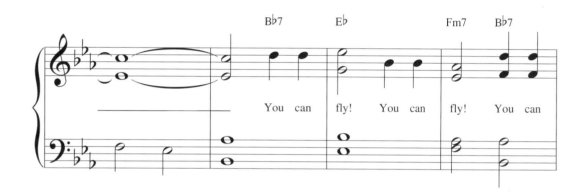

bir - ies can. At least it's worth a try. _____

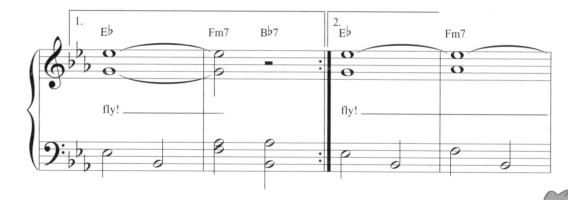

_____ You can fly! You can fly! You can

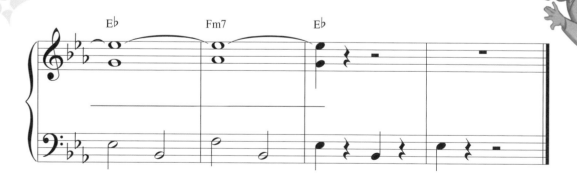

fly! _____ fly! _____

WRITTEN IN THE STARS

from Elton John and Tim Rice's *Aida*

Music by ELTON JOHN
Lyrics by TIM RICE

(Male:) Here I am to tell ___ you we can nev-er meet a-gain.

Sim-ple real-ly, ___ is-n't it? ___ A word or two and then a

life-time of not know-ing where or how or why or when. You

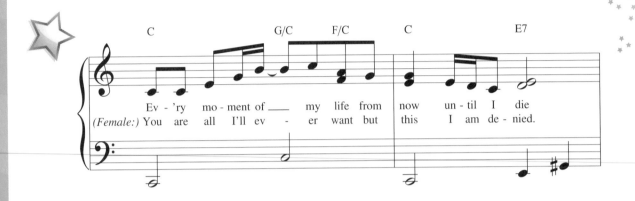

Ev - 'ry mo - ment of ___ my life from now un - til I die
(Female:) You are all I'll ev - er want but this I am de - nied.

I will think ___ or dream of you ___ and fail ___ to un - der - stand ___ how a
Some-times in ___ my dark-est thoughts ___ I wish ___ I nev-er learned ___ what it

per - fect love can be ___ con - found - ed out of hand. *(Both:)* Is it
is to be in love ___ and have that love re - turned.

writ - ten in the stars? ___ Are we pay - ing for some crime? ___ Is that

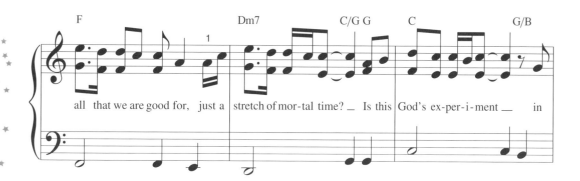

all that we are good for, just a | stretch of mor-tal time? __ Is this | God's ex-per-i-ment __ in

which we have no say? __ In | which we're giv-en par-a-dise, but | on - ly for a day. __

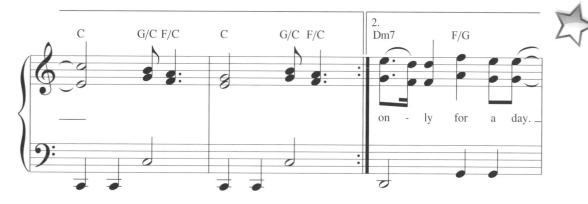

__ | | on - ly for a day.

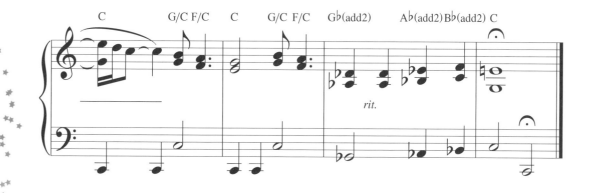

rit.